THE *OTHER* PLAYBOOK

Brand Lessons Every Student-Athlete Needs
(But No One Teaches)

AMIT CHITRE

The *Other* Playbook:
Brand Lessons Every Student-Athlete Needs (But No One Teaches)

ISBN Paperback: 979-8-89576-124-3

Published by:

"As a former D1 hockey national champion, I've seen firsthand how success doesn't just come from talent — it comes from mindset, leadership, and how you carry yourself on and off the ice. *The Other Playbook* gives our players a competitive edge beyond the rink. These principles are a core part of our team's development, because building your brand isn't ego — it's preparation for life."

Matt Alvey
NCAA Division I Men's Hockey National Champion,
Lake Superior State University
Boston Bruins Draft Pick
Hockey Head Coach, Albany Academy

"Amit does an excellent job with *The Other Playbook* on creating a usable tool belt for student-athletes of all ages to set themselves up for success. As a former college and pro athlete, and a current basketball coach, I found so many tangible pieces of wisdom for young people to prepare for their future in this book. At the same time, I enjoyed the read and found great lessons for my own growth!"

Jack Leasure
Men's Basketball Big South Conference Player of the Year,
Coastal Carolina University
New Zealand National Basketball League (NBL) Scoring Champ
Pro Basketball Skills Trainer

"*The Other Playbook* is exactly what today's student-athletes need. It bridges the gap between performance and personal growth, helping athletes understand that their brand is more than stats — it's how they lead, show up, and leave a legacy. We're excited to use this as a resource to support our athletes beyond the game."

Megan V. Buchanan
Senior Associate Director of Athletics, Skidmore College
Athletic Hall of Fame, University at Albany

"*The Other Playbook* is a valuable resource for young student-athletes looking to develop and market their personal brand. To my knowledge, no other book on the market exists that breaks down the complexities of personal branding into clear, relevant, and actionable steps for this audience. I would highly recommend *The Other Playbook* to any student-athlete preparing for the college recruiting process or before stepping into their first professional opportunity. It's not just a book or workbook, it's a roadmap to a future full of clarity, purpose, and success."

Michael Tanke
Head Men's Soccer Coach, Canisius University

"*The Other Playbook* is a great tool for all athletes to have in their back pocket. This book allowed me to take a step back and reevaluate how I think of myself as an athlete, coach, and leader. It also helped me understand how I want others, such as sponsors, to perceive me. Every athlete should have this book in their toolbox to help them grow personally and professionally."

Brooke Austin
NCAA Division I Women's Tennis National Champion,
University of Florida
Director, Digital Business, United States Tennis Association (USTA)

"Throughout my career, first as a professional athlete and now as a college coach, I've had the privilege of working with many distinguished teams and individuals. I've noticed that those who elevated themselves from good to great and achieved success consistently recognized the crucial role of ownership in their development, both in sports and in life. *The Other Playbook* provides a detailed strategy for student-athletes aiming to take charge of their story and brand, pursuing excellence at every stage of their student-athlete experience."

Krystian Witkowski
Head Men's Soccer Coach, Fairfield University

For Dad, who always said I should,
Mom, who always believed I could,
And Mona, who always knew I would.

Also, for my boys, the reason I finally did.

TABLE OF CONTENTS

PREFACE

The vice president of a Fortune 500 company asked me to present my Personal Brand Development Training to a handful of his best employees. They were all high performers with the potential to grow in their careers, but they needed advice on developing leadership and communication skills. My training would teach them to define what they stand for, both in and out of the workplace. A strong, clearly defined personal brand would build confidence and help them stand out from their peers. The VP believed that with the proper training, he could promote these individuals to high-level positions within the year.

And he was right.

A year later, the same vice president reported that several managers from the training had been promoted to new positions. By defining what they stand for, these individuals developed a brand that helped advance their careers. But that's not the point of this story.

As I was putting the final touches on that training session, carefully rehearsing my slides and practicing the exercises I would lead the participants through, I realized I needed an audience. For such an interactive presentation, I wanted to practice asking questions, listening to responses, and leading activities. And so, I recruited my children.

My three boys were playing basketball in the driveway and were quite reluctant to come inside, but eventually, they agreed to humor me. As they lined up on the couch to listen, I assumed the content would be too complex for them. My youngest was in junior high, and the two older boys were in high school. But a funny thing happened once I launched into the presentation.

The light bulb went off.

I had spent many hours of my career training young professionals on the value of defining their personal brands. I went from company to company to lay the groundwork for these skills. But as I looked at my children, each with their own goals and ambitions for the future, I wondered, "*Why do we wait so long to teach these life skills?*"

Within the next few years, my sons will meet with coaches, recruiters, counselors, teachers, employers, admissions officers, and many more. They would have important decisions to make about the people they wanted to be, and others would make important decisions about them. People they know, and even those they don't, would make judgments based on who they believe my sons are as people. And many of those decisions would impact their futures.

I had been training career professionals, but what if I was training the *wrong audience?*

I realised that young adults, especially student-athletes, have far more to gain from personal brand development than those Fortune 500 employees. That's because personal brand development isn't just a career skill- It's a *life* skill. Understanding and developing your personal brand will help you promote your best qualities. You'll be in control of how you're perceived by others. Furthermore, you'll create a positive, lasting impression on the people most important to you.

This isn't about creating a look or a logo. It's about defining and creating the best version of *you* by understanding what you stand for and taking the necessary steps to build on those strengths. Your brand lies within you. It's waiting to be uncovered and unleashed. Let's go find it.

INTRODUCTION

During elementary school, shopping for shoes was a painful experience.

My parents would take me to the shoe store, and I would walk straight to the Nike aisle. I remember surveying the new high tops, awed by the colors and that crisp, iconic swoosh on the side of the shoe. I could already hear my friends as I walked into class the next day:

Whoa. New Nikes!

Nice shoes, Amit.

Of course, I'd always snap back to reality when my parents called out to me from the next aisle.

"Try these on," they said, more of a demand than a request, as they handed me a pair of Kangaroos. (You probably haven't heard of these sneakers. But, believe me, they were as bad as you imagine.)

"No one in school wears these," I'd complain, but I'd always shuffle my way to the bench and slump down, slipping my feet out of my faded, worn pair of 'Roos' to dutifully try on the new ones.

Middle school was a little better. My 'Roos' were replaced by Converse—a more recognizable sneaker brand. They still weren't the flashy Nikes I dreamed of walking into school with, but at least my friends wouldn't tease me about what was on my feet.

I was in high school when I finally accepted my fate. With a fresh pair of Reeboks on my feet, I had upgraded from the Kangaroos of elementary school, but by now, I understood my parents would never buy me the latest Nikes.

It's easy to assume that price was the only factor in their decision. The shoes I wanted sold for thirty times more than what they cost to make, and the price point was far higher than the shoes they ended up buying for me.

But it wasn't about the money.

It was about the brand.

My parents and I had a fundamental difference in the way we viewed that Nike swoosh.

I saw the Swoosh as a symbol of success, popularity, and elite status. Michael Jordan (still the greatest basketball player of all time—sorry, LeBron fans) wore Nike. Many of my friends at school wore them. I wanted to wear the Nike brand.

My parents saw the brand differently. To them, it was a symbol of excess spending. As hard-working immigrants on a tight budget, they saw Nikes as an unnecessary luxury. If other brands did the same job of protecting your feet, why pay so much more for the Swoosh?

Given my childhood sneaker desperation, you would think I would remember the first pair of Nike sneakers I bought myself. I don't. At some point in high school, I earned and saved enough money to buy them. But I can't tell you exactly when it happened or even what the sneakers looked like. I can't even tell you if my friends reacted like I imagined they would during all of those previous sneaker shopping trips.

What I can tell you is that my commitment to the brand continued. I bought Nikes exclusively through college and young adulthood. It was my way of living the dream I had so desperately longed for in my childhood. Those Nikes made me feel cool, important, and relevant. I wore them because I wanted everyone else to *see* that Nike Swoosh on the side of the sneaker. I wore them because of the *brand*.

THE BIGGER PICTURE

At this point, you may be thinking: *How does a story about sneakers help me gain a competitive advantage in sports, school, and life?* My experience with the Nike swoosh offers lessons about brand value, loyalty, perception, influence, and more. You probably have similar experiences.

All you have to do is look at your clothes, the backpack next to you, and the cell phone nearby to understand that we don't only choose products for what they *do*. We choose products because of how they make us feel. How many of us have felt compelled to wear a specific brand to the gym or class? How many of us use our gear, our cars, and our belongings to present a picture to our friends, family, and even strangers, giving them a hint of who we are before we even open our mouths?

Well, I'm here to tell you that you have more in common with a sneaker, a cell phone, or a sports drink than you might think. To understand this, you must accept a simple but controversial premise: *You are a product.*

Think of any industry: clothes, hotels, restaurants, energy drinks, sports franchises, cosmetics—each is filled with companies astutely aware of how their brand is positioned and perceived by you. You are no different, with "customers" making judgments about you based on how they perceive your brand.

Brands don't succeed without someone doing the work behind the scenes. Businesses spend billions of dollars to study, measure, and develop brands to capture your attention and win you over. Just as they put in the work to craft their brand and products, you too must be intentional about your brand.

YOUR BRAND PLAYBOOK

You don't step onto the court or the field for a big contest without running through drills, reviewing tape, and making a game plan. This is why I have developed a step-by-step, easy-to-follow guide to help you understand, define, develop, and protect the very valuable asset of your brand.

This book is designed to be your playbook, and the activities and questions in these chapters will help you prepare just as you would for that big game. But like with any other competition or test, you have to put in the work. You'll create an action plan specifically designed to help you succeed, focused on three core principles:

1. Understand the Brand
2. Build the Brand
3. Protect the Brand

Whether you're seeking a college scholarship, applying for that big job, or trying to impress a coach or a recruiter, the skills in this book will stretch and strengthen your brand muscles. By following the steps, you will learn how to develop your brand and build the best version of you in sports, in the classroom, and in every other aspect of your life.

HOW TO USE THIS BOOK

This book is designed as a workbook, meant to be a hands-on process for building your brand. The activities can be followed by individuals or teams working to define and build their best attributes as part of a holistic, comprehensive training program. To get the most out of this book, readers should spend time with each chapter and complete the suggested activities before moving to the next step in their action plan. Each chapter also ends with helpful discussion questions, which can be answered individually or in a team setting.

Remember: Just as you work hard to build your skills on the court, on the field, or in any competition, you must work hard to define, grow, and strengthen your brand. While brand building is an individual task, with each person having unique brand attributes, working with a team on this book can keep you motivated and inspired.

So lace up those Nikes, or whatever sneaker you like, and get ready to build the best version of you!

PART ONE:
UNDERSTAND THE BRAND

"It doesn't matter what your background is and where you come from, if you have dreams and goals, that's all that matters."

—Serena Williams

Professional tennis player, Olympic gold medalist, 23-time Grand Slam singles champion

YOU ARE A PRODUCT

THE ATHLETE'S JOURNEY

Lewis Hamilton is one of the world's premier race car drivers. As of March 2025, he holds the record for the most wins, pole positions, and podium finishes in Formula 1[1]. He broke barriers in the world of motorsports as the first black driver to compete in the highest class of international racing, and he continues to shatter records in his career. In addition to his skills on the track, Hamilton has amassed a wide following, often credited with making the viewership of Formula 1 more diverse. He is also an outspoken advocate for social issues and has become an international fashion icon.

Let's take a moment to imagine a day in the life of Hamilton during the height of his racing career. After enjoying a healthy breakfast to fuel him for a race day, he turns to his closet. He knows paparazzi will photograph him arriving at the track, and he needs to film some content for social media later that day. He carefully chooses his clothing to promote his sponsors, knowing the logos on his shirt or hat have value.

As he leaves his house, he may have his pick of cars in the garage. He scans his options, imagining what people will think as he pulls into his parking space. If a fan, a competitor, or a coach catches sight of the Maserati or the Porsche, will they be impressed, intimidated, or put off by the flash of extravagance? Or perhaps Hamilton chooses a Ferrari to please his current racing team.

The speedway is covered with advertisements and endless billboards surrounding the track. Similarly, as Hamilton suits up for the race, he puts on a racing suit covered with logos and branding. These racing suits are fire-retardant garments meant to keep athletes safe in the event of a crash, but over the years, they've become walking advertisements. Hamilton has accepted that promoting companies and wearing their brands is a part of his sport, so he doesn't think much of it as he slips into the car and drives to the starting line.

Everywhere you look, and on every step of this journey from the moment Hamilton wakes up to the moment the light flashes green to start the race, there is a brand.

The sports world is inundated with advertisements and sponsorships. We can watch any televised event and easily count a dozen companies that have purchased the opportunity to compete for our attention. But there's one brand we didn't mention in the athlete's journey, and it may be the most important: *The athlete.*

Keep in mind, the athlete's brand didn't magically appear once they became famous, though fame certainly makes them more visible and recognizable. But athletes often cultivate their brands and what they stand for, long before they find success in their sport. You could argue that their brand is precisely what enables them to achieve that success. To unlock and unleash your full brand potential, you must first realize a concept that many student-athletes overlook: **You are a product.**

It's time to think of yourself like that bottle of soda on the billboard or the newest cell phone from a commercial, because whether you realize it or not, you already have a brand.

WHAT IS A BRAND?

Before we begin developing your brand value, it's important to understand what "brand" actually means. The word comes from a surprisingly simple origin. At first, these early examples might seem very distant from the logos and names we see in media or on store shelves. But when we look closer, we can find a logical path from the beginning of the word to the brands of today.

You are likely familiar with the concept of branding cattle, where ranchers use hot metal to burn a mark into the skin of their livestock. The mark was unique and permanent, allowing the ranchers to formalize their ownership and ensure no one else could claim (or steal) their property. This practice continued as civilizations evolved. When traders sent goods by ship, wagon, or train, they often branded the containers to identify them. Just like the ranchers before them, traders wanted to prevent theft and establish ownership, and they did this by marking their products.

It wasn't long before the brands themselves began to gain value.

The ranchers and traders didn't set out to design a logo or "mark" that would hold value on its own. They simply wanted to protect their assets. But we can see how these marks took on their own identities. In any competitive marketplace, someone (or something) will always emerge as superior. It stands to reason that the rancher with the best cattle will gain attention, as will the identifying mark on the animal's side. As a rancher's popularity grew, so did that rancher's brand.

Those early businessmen soon learned that their brands had value. Anyone who recognized their mark would feel something based on their previous experiences with that rancher or trader. Over time, the brand served as a shorthand to tell the customer what that product stood for.

Fast-forward to today. How has the definition of "brand" evolved from marking the skin of cattle? A man widely considered the "Father of Modern Advertising" has the answer.

THE SUM OF ITS PARTS

So, what is a brand?

"The intangible sum of a product's attributes: its name, packaging, and price, its history, its reputation, and the way it's advertised."
—**David Ogilvy,** Author of *On Advertising*

British advertising pioneer David Ogilvy found great success in his career by focusing on branding. His definition of the word shows his belief that a brand is much more than a name or a logo. Instead, it is a composite of many elements, all working together to form the whole. A brand includes the elements we can see, such as the name, packaging, and colors of the product, but it also includes elements that aren't as obvious. It includes the history of the brand, its reputation, and its advertising.

Let's remember the example we discussed in the introduction regarding shoes. When you walk the aisles of a shoe store, you will encounter rows and rows of shoes, all of which will protect and cover your feet. But as you view the names and logos on the shoes, you will inevitably think about much more than the shoe's utility. You'll remember that commercial you saw featuring your favorite athlete. You might think about an article you read outlining the company's commitment to sustainability. Or you might avoid a particular brand because of recent news stories about labor conditions in their factories. These are all elements that make up a brand.

Most importantly, the value of the brand lies in how *you* have experienced it. In other words, how do all of those touchpoints– from the price, to the celebrity spokesperson, to how much you enjoyed (or hated) using it, to what your friends say about it, to everything else in between–how does that collective "intangible sum" make you feel?

THE POWER OF A BRAND

Brand value doesn't happen by accident. It is carefully cultivated by companies that spend billions of dollars to help ensure you feel a certain way when you try their product. Marketing executives invest a lot of time thinking about the music, lighting, and smell when you walk into a Starbucks. Similarly, the tones you hear when you put on your wireless headphones or start your laptop were specifically created to elicit an emotional response. Companies spend significant resources to craft how their products might make you feel.

Let's try an exercise to demonstrate this point. Take a look at the logos below. Do you recognize these brands? If so, what do they mean to you? What do you *feel* when you see them? Spend a minute answering the questions below each logo.

1. Have you used this product? In what way?

2. How did it make you feel?

3. How would you describe athletes who wear this product?

This company represents a 33 billion dollar business.

1. Do you associate this logo with a particular sport or activity?

2. How does it make you feel?

3. How would you describe the product?

This may be one of the world's most recognizable logos.

1. Can you remember the first time you tasted McDonald's fries?

2. How did it make you feel?

3. Now think about the most recent time you went to McDonald's. How did that experience differ from your first time?

There is no right or wrong answer for each of these examples, but there are a few important lessons to remember.

First, your answer may be quite different than a teammate's or friend's because you may each have very different experiences with the brands. For example, you may be indifferent about Under Armour, but your friend loves them after winning a free pair of Under Armour sneakers in a contest. Your teammate may be brand-loyal to Lululemon because she loves the athleisure style fit, but you may find their products too expensive. Or you may love McDonald's fries, but your friend may think they taste too salty. Different people will view brands differently.

Next, your own perceptions of a brand may change over time. Maybe you loved McDonald's as a child, but now you are more health-conscious and feel differently about the brand. Or five years from now, you'll likely earn more money than you do today, and you may prefer purchasing the higher quality, more expensive Lululemon.

Finally, despite a company's best efforts to influence how you feel, you still may feel differently than the company intends. But that doesn't change the fact that companies are hyper-thoughtful and deliberate in how they present their products to you, the customer.

Keep these points in mind—we will return to them and discuss how these lessons affect your personal brand a bit later on.

THE PERSONAL BRAND

Just as products have brands, so do people. This is what we mean by a Personal Brand. Your personal brand is the way other people perceive you. More specifically, it is how your "intangible sum" makes them feel.

Let's go through a similar exercise, using people instead of companies, to understand what we mean.

1. How do you feel about Simone Biles?
2. What assumptions can we make about her?
3. Biles famously stepped away from international competition in 2021, citing mental health concerns[2]. Did that change your opinion of her? If so, how?

1. Do you recognize this athlete?
2. What do you think he is famous for?
3. Even if you don't recognize him, what can we learn about his brand from this image?

1. What's the first thing that comes to your mind when you see this athlete?
2. How has Tiger Woods's brand changed over time?
3. If you have followed the ups and downs of his career and personal life, how do you feel now about Tiger?

1. What is this athlete best known for?
2. What words would you use to describe her?
3. If you owned a women's clothing brand, would this be an athlete you want associated with your company? If your company sold cars instead, would you choose the same athlete? Why or why not?

Reflecting on these sports stars may raise strong opinions or emotions that shape what you think these athletes represent.

Chances are those opinions are based not only on their trophies, championships, Olympic medals, buzzer beaters, or game-winning plays. Your feelings are also formed by what they say in press conferences, news articles you read about them, and things you see posted on social media. You might also have strong opinions about the actions or choices these athletes made when they weren't playing the game. Taking a knee, getting arrested, advocating for mental health issues, or fighting for equal pay may even be the most decisive factor in your judgment of the athlete.

Just as a company's brand is much more than its products, these athletes' personal brands are much more than their athletic ability. The same goes for you. It's important to understand that many elements go into your personal brand, and most don't involve game statistics or muscle mass. The attributes of David Ogilvy can apply to people as much as they apply to products: name, history, and reputation.

EVERYONE HAS A BRAND

We have established that we all make assumptions about athletes as soon as we hear their names. But what about athletes who don't have name recognition? If we haven't watched them compete, read news articles about them, or followed them on social media, do they still have a brand? The answer, of course, is yes.

Take a look at the picture above. What do you feel when you look at this picture? This snapshot in time doesn't provide a lot of details, but let's imagine a few scenarios. Maybe he's frustrated that his quarterback threw an interception. Maybe he's exhausted after a long play. Maybe he's upset at himself for dropping a pass. Whatever the situation, what message does his body language communicate? Frustration? Fatigue? Disappointment? Can you imagine a positive scenario associated with this body language?

Even though we don't know this athlete, we make judgments about their brand before we know their name. We all do it naturally. As soon as you looked at this picture, you started making judgments based on appearances alone.

Similarly, I'm guessing you probably haven't met Simone Biles, Jake Paul, Tiger Woods, or Megan Rapinoe. But you still have opinions about them, perhaps even strong opinions. People who have never met you are forming opinions about you. Before they learn your name, they will observe you. They will look at your appearance, your actions, and the way you carry yourself, and they will make judgments. How do you want them to feel?

THE FINAL SCORE

In this chapter, we explored the origins of the word "brand" from its earliest days as a tool for ranchers and traders. We learned how these markings gained value, eventually representing much more than a product. David Ogilvy's definition showed us that brands are made of many parts, all working together to form a whole.

From here, we examined the concept of personal brand value. Companies invest significant resources to influence how you feel about their products. Athletes, like products, also have brand value which is far more than their achievement in sport.

Your brand value lies in the "intangible sum" of your actions, social media posts, speech, appearance, and so much more. These elements are separate from your ability to play the game, but they can sometimes have disproportionate impacts on how you are perceived.

Now that you understand how you are a product, it only makes sense to think about how you want your product to be perceived. Just as companies influence customers by creating the best brand experience, you can influence how your customers feel by creating the best version of you. But first, we'll need to tackle an important question: *Who are your customers?*

CHAPTER 1 EXERCISE

Choose three athletes from any sport and answer the questions below for each athlete.

1. Athlete 1:_____

   a. How would you describe their brand?

   _____

   _____

   _____

   _____

   _____

   b. *Why* would you describe their brand that way?

   _____

   _____

   _____

   _____

   _____

c. Do any of the brand attributes resonate outside of the athlete's sport? How and why?

_____

_____

_____

_____

_____

_____

2. Athlete 2:_____

   a. How would you describe their brand?

   _____

   _____

   _____

   _____

   _____

   _____

   b. *Why* would you describe their brand that way?

   _____

_____

_____

_____

_____

_____

c. Do any of the brand attributes resonate outside of the athlete's sport? How and why?

_____

_____

_____

_____

_____

_____

3. Athlete 3:_____

a. How would you describe their brand?

_____

_____

_____

_____

_____

_____

b. *Why* would you describe their brand that way?

_____

_____

_____

_____

_____

_____

c. Do any of the brand attributes resonate outside of the athlete's sport? How and why?

_____

_____

_____

_____

_____

_____

4. Why can you form opinions about these athletes even though you've never met them?

_____

_____

_____

_____

_____

_____

CHAPTER 2

YOU HAVE CUSTOMERS

THE ATHLETE'S JOURNEY

By 2009, Michael Phelps had already made a name for himself as one of the greatest Olympic swimmers in history, having won eight gold medals at the 2008 Beijing Olympics[1]. But only six months later, Phelps took an unexpected loss, and it didn't come in the pool. A tabloid newspaper published a photo of Phelps at a party using a bong[2]. The impact was significant.

Smoking pot at a party, months after the Olympics concluded, may seem like a small controversy compared to other issues athletes get caught up in today. After all, Phelps was a 23-year-old athlete who had worked hard at breaking records in nearly every event he swam in. Would people care if he blew off a little steam, or in this case, marijuana, at a college party? Probably not his teammates and friends. But others viewed this action very negatively, especially his sponsors and USA Swimming.

In addition to being a role model for young fans and athletes, Phelps partnered with companies during his Olympic run. These included household names such as Kellogg's, Speedo, and Visa. Some of these companies did not appreciate seeing their spokesperson engage in an activity that was contrary to their business values. The Kellogg's Company even dropped their sponsorship and decided not to renew their contract with Phelps. A spokesperson for the brand said that

"Michael's most recent behavior is not consistent with the image of Kellogg's."[3]

In addition to losing this deal, USA Swimming, the governing body for competitive swimming in the U.S., suspended Phelps for three months. The organization decided to "send a strong message to Michael because he disappointed so many people, particularly the hundreds of thousands of USA Swimming kids who look up to him."[3] This single photograph had major implications for Phelps's reputation and his bank account. Two very important organizations made public statements denouncing his behavior and even cut ties with him completely.

Phelps learned perhaps the most important lesson of his career: Know all of your customers.

Athletes have many people watching them, and not just on television. There are fans at live events, coaches and teammates at practice, and companies that look at sponsorship opportunities to drive sales. All of these people are potential customers for the athlete. Someone like Phelps can earn a massive income from sponsorship deals, but that means he can lose huge amounts if he disappoints those sponsors. Phelps clearly wasn't thinking about this when he chose to smoke at a party and, worse, pose for photographs while doing it. In an interview, Phelps admitted, "It's a bad judgment. I can learn from it."[3]

So, what can you learn from Phelps's mistake? Just as Michael Phelps has customers, so do you. It's the logical conclusion from the idea we discussed earlier: you are a product. No product can succeed without customers buying it. So, if you are a product, it follows that you also have customers, just like your favorite cereal or a piece of sports equipment. It's up to you to keep these customers in mind as you build your personal brand.

WHAT IS A CUSTOMER?

Let's consider a company that is launching a new product. Long before the product hits the shelves, the company must think about its customers. Is this product designed for an eighteen-year-old male high school student? Or is it designed for a thirty-two-year-old mother? As you can imagine, these two people are very different. They obviously have different genders and ages. They are also at different points in their lives, with different priorities, habits, likes, and dislikes. It stands to reason that the products they buy will be different, too.

To have success with a product, companies must spend time determining who their customers are. The term *demographic* is often used in these situations. Organizations narrow in on a specific section of the population and target their products to these people. By understanding what demographic the product speaks to, companies know where to put their advertising dollars. For example, if you're trying to reach an eighteen-year-old high school student, you probably won't market your product in the newspaper. Similarly, the thirty-two-year-old mother is not likely to be playing many video games, so you would not put ads for your product on gaming websites.

Even though people aren't literally buying you, it's important to remember that you have a personal brand just like these products. And that means you also have customers. Let's apply the two demographics above to you:

- **Eighteen-year-old high school student:** Perhaps this person is your teammate or a younger player on the team. When he looks at you, what does he see? How do your words, actions, and appearance influence his opinion of you?

- **Thirty-two-year-old mother:** This person might be a coach or a teacher. She might be a blogger covering local sports. When she hears your words and sees your actions and appearance, what does she see? How is her opinion different from your teammates?

Both individuals will judge you based on how you look, your attitude, and how you interact with others. Even if they don't know you personally, they will make assumptions about you. These two customers will engage with you in different ways and, as such, will receive you (the product) through different eyes. So why is it important to realize this? Well, once we understand that we have different customers, we can pay closer attention to how they perceive our brand and avoid making the same mistake as Michael Phelps.

LISTING YOUR CUSTOMERS

Now that you're looking at the people around you as customers, let's think about how many of them you interact with as a student-athlete. You have teachers in the classroom, friends and teammates in the lunchroom, and your coaches, trainers, and guidance counselors after school. If we expand beyond the walls of the school, we can include your parents, employers and co-workers, family, fans, and leaders or members of your religious or community groups. You may also identify some future customers: college admissions departments, coaches of professional teams, recruiters, or sponsors. Each of these is a customer making judgments about you, the product.

With so many different customers, how can you possibly please them all?

Simple: you can't.

It's nearly impossible to create a brand that every customer will relate to. Remember that organizations often focus on only one or two demographics when they try to make their product successful. Two customers will often perceive a product differently: one group will love it while the other completely ignores it. It's the same with people. Imagine you get thrown out of a game for fighting with a referee. Maybe you were standing up for a teammate after a bad call, which makes your team proud of you. But a fan in the stands might see this action as unsportsmanlike. We don't bring up this example to pass judgment on the action, but to show how two people can view this argument with the referee in very different ways.

Some of your favorite athletes, movie stars, and musicians have found very specific demographics to speak to. Some comedians always stick to funny movies and don't venture into drama. Often, this is because they understand what their audience wants. And it can be the same for athletes. Think about athletes like Serena Williams or Sabrina Ionescu, who have a large female fan base. Many of the products they choose to align themselves with or the commercials they are featured in will also speak to that female audience. It isn't necessary to speak to *every customer* to find success. But your product must speak to *the right customers*.

THE CUSTOMER EXPERIENCE

Think about the different customers in your life and why they want to engage with you. Are they a teammate counting on you to be at your best on the field? Are they an admissions officer looking to see if you will fit into their university? Are they an employer wondering if you have the skills and mindset to help their company? Are they a fan who wants to be entertained? Once you understand these "*Whys*," you can determine which customer is most important to you.

In marketing, companies often think about the customer experience. This is how the customers engage with the products and how the products make them feel. Remember that you are a product. It's important to recognize that different customers will perceive your product in different ways. Your teammate may like your brand (how you make them feel) because you crack jokes and make them laugh at practice. But your coach may be trying to explain an important lesson, and he finds your jokes distracting. They have different "*Whys*."

Knowing that your customers perceive you in different ways isn't necessarily a negative. You might decide to prioritize your teammates over your coach, but you should ask if that is the best decision for your overall brand. When you think about your long-term goals for sports, school, and life, which customers will help you get there? Which customers are the most influential? Who has the most power or sway to help you succeed?

Let's say you decide that you want to impress your coaches and your teachers. To do this, you must put yourself in their shoes. Think about what they are looking for in a product. Take a moment to see the world through the coach's eyes and make some informed decisions about what traits are important to them. Take some time to think about the customer experience. The sooner you start looking outside yourself to analyze what others see, the faster you'll be able to create the product your customers are looking for.

We have established what brand value means and how we, as products, have customers. Once we identify which customers are most important to us, we must think about what we want their customer experience to be. In other words, how do we want those customers to feel about us? Remember, companies spend a lot of time thinking about how you feel when using their products. It's time for you to do the same.

THE FINAL SCORE

In this chapter, we discussed companies focusing on specific demographics to sell their products. We came to understand that different customers will view products in different ways, and the companies must adjust their marketing efforts accordingly. Since you are also a product, you also have many customers.

We took a moment to think about the many customers you have around you. You might start with people you interact with at school, but then you can expand your list to those in your home, community groups, religious organizations, and at your job. You can even consider future customers you hope to attract, such as college scouts, fans, or company sponsors. With so many customers, it's impossible to please all of them. Two customers might view the very same product in two very different ways.

Understanding your customers' *why* will help you prioritize the customers in your life. Now that you know who your customers are, *can you create a game plan for shaping how they feel about you?*

CHAPTER 2 EXERCISE

List 5-10 of your "customers" below:

1.	6.
2.	7.
3.	8.
4.	9.
5.	10.

These are the people who engage with you in different aspects of your life. Once you have listed your customers, answer the questions below:

1. Would all of these customers view you as a product in the same way? Why or why not?

_____

_____

_____

_____

_____

_____

2. Which customers are most important to you? Why? Prioritize this list.

TOP FIVE CUSTOMERS
1.
2.
3.
4.
5.

3. How might this list change in the next 6 months? 1 year? 5 years?

_____

_____

_____

_____

_____

_____

PART TWO:

BUILD THE BRAND

"Excellence is not a singular act but a habit. You are what you do repeatedly."

—Shaquille O'Neal

Professional basketball player, 4-time NBA champion, 15-time NBA All-Star, Olympic gold medalist

DETERMINE YOUR VALUES

THE ATHLETE'S JOURNEY

The Triathlon World Championship is a grueling competition-- a series of swimming, biking, and running events to crown the world's greatest triathlete. In September of 2016, the series' final race came down to a stunning finish. In the last 500 meters, Henri Shoeman sprinted past the two runners in front of him to win in dramatic fashion[1].

Despite his win, Shoeman became almost an afterthought. Media, spectators, and fans worldwide were more interested in Jonathan and Alistair Brownlee, brothers from England who finished in second and third place. The two were triathlon legends with Alistair having won gold and Jonathan taking silver at the Rio Olympics earlier that year[2]. This time, Jonathan was leading in the final stretch - until his body began to fail him.

With the finish line in sight, heat exhaustion set in. Jonathan began to stumble and could barely push forward. As Alistair caught up to his distressed brother, he had to make a split-second decision: finish the race and claim first place, or sacrifice the win to help his brother. Despite endless hours of extreme training, rigid diet restrictions, and countless other sacrifices to be the best at his sport, his decision was clear.

Alistair rushed to his brother's side. He held him up, keeping Jonny on his feet. And then Alistair set his sights on the finish line. His brother leaned on him as they made slow but steady progress, Jonny's legs barely supporting the weight of his body. Along the way, Henri Shoeman passed the brothers to claim the win.

As the brothers approached the finish line, Alistair pushed Jonathon ahead, giving his brother second place while he took third. "Mum wouldn't have been happy if I'd left Jonny behind," he told a reporter after the race[3].

Alistair probably didn't expect all of the attention that followed. After all, he was already an Olympic gold medalist. But the world responded differently to this race than to his Olympic win. There was something about his display of brotherhood that spoke to people and made them sit up and watch. At this moment, Alistair showed what made him different from other athletes. He lived his values and, by losing the race, he solidified his brand as one of the world's greatest triathletes.

WHAT SETS A PRODUCT APART?

Before companies can sell a product, they must understand what the product does and who it will benefit. Let's take the example of a baseball bat. High school and college athletes have hundreds of choices when it comes to bats. They are made of different materials, come in different weights and lengths, and have different grips for the athlete's hands. Then, outside of the structure and form of the product, there are thousands of different colors, logos, and designs to choose from.

With baseball being the national pastime, you might think the bat market is already saturated. After all, how can we still be innovating for a sport that has been around since the 1800s? But even in a saturated market, companies must think about why the customer chooses their bat over a competitor's similar product. Is the bat of higher quality? Less expensive? Does it feature a new, more comfortable design? Or has the brand partnered with a local artist to provide eye-popping graphics? (Maybe it's a "Torpedo Bat" which the New York Yankees brought to fame in the Spring of 2025[4]!) Companies must understand *why* customers are responding to their products.

Now, imagine you are a Chief Marketing Officer trying to understand why customers are buying your baseball bats. But instead of bats, let's change the product to *you*. Why should the customers you identified in the last chapter choose you over anyone else? Let's give them a few reasons that set you apart.

The great news is that you don't need to do any work to *create* your uniqueness. You are already your own, individual product. Your skills, appearance, personality, and values all work together to create a blend no one possesses. *You* will be better at being *you* than anyone else around you.

WHAT DO YOU VALUE?

We started this chapter by discussing what your customers will see. Our story about the Brownlee brothers reinforces the idea that customers watch your actions and listen to your words, and they make judgments about you. Alistair Brownlee had no control over how the spectators, news media, and fans would view him when he lost the race to carry his brother across the finish line. But there is something he *did* have control over: his values.

Your values are shaped by many things, including your parents or your upbringing, your coaches, your community, experiences at school or in your religious organization, and your interactions with friends, family, and strangers. Believe it or not, your values affect how you play sports and how you speak with your friends. They determine how you talk to your coach or what time you show up at a meet. Values affect every aspect of your life and, therefore, your brand. So it shouldn't be surprising to hear that your *values* are the building blocks we must use to create your brand. In other words, before we can choose what we want our customers to see, we must identify our unique personal values.

Here are a few values to get you thinking. Of course, this list is not exhaustive. There are hundreds of values we could list, and the important thing is to choose words that speak to you. What words spark energy and excitement when you read them? Which do you identify with, and which do you *want* to identify with in the future?

Bold	Friendly	Spiritual
Helpful	Authoritative	Studious
Serious	Strong	Positive
Adventurous	Whimsical	Hard-working
Imaginative	Cooperative	Resourceful
Neat	Collaborative	Respectful
Mature	Humble	Controversial
Dependable	Energetic	Edgy

You can find a longer list of values in Appendix A of this book on Page 122.

So, how do you identify your values? Some of them may come to mind very easily. Others you will need to reflect on. Values often come from a combination of strengths and aspirations, so let's think about both of these categories, starting with the values you may already possess. These are the things coaches or teammates say about us or what we may recognize in ourselves. Something you are very good at might be closely related to one of your values. For example, if you cheer for your teammates while sitting on the bench or the sidelines and enjoy lifting your teammates up when they are down, you may value being collaborative, motivational, kind, or positive.

VALUES IN OTHERS

Another way to think about your own values is to reflect on what you see in others. Think about a great team captain or coach you really connect with. What do you admire in that person? How do they present themselves? Now, think about a teammate you did not get along with. What values did that person have that you did *not* agree with? Have you had a teammate who always showed up late to practice or only cared about their own personal stats?

You can go through the same exercise with sports figures you look up to or dislike. Choose one of your favorite athletes. What is it you like about them? Is it their tenacity on the basketball court? Is it their kindness on the soccer pitch? Are they serious and intense about their game and their training, or do they take a more youthful, fun approach? Perhaps you relate to an athlete because they are humble, or, on the other hand, you may find their controversial and edgy persona an exciting and compelling attribute.

Think about the values you already possess and the values you hope to show in the future, and create a broad list. This is the first step in determining our attributes, or what we want our customers to see. We must understand what we believe in before we start telling other people what to think about us. *This is not an easy exercise, especially if you are not used to thinking about yourself.* So let's first see how it works for someone else.

VALUES IN ACTION

Imagine a freshman lacrosse player, Jesse, who is new to a college team. He is dedicated to the sport and wants to succeed over the next four years, but he isn't sure where he fits in with all the players who have been working together for seasons. With several new players and many upperclassmen on the team, Jesse finds it difficult to stand out in front of his coaches and teammates.

Jesse has already spent some time considering his values. After reflecting on his strengths, what past coaches have said about him, and what he sees as positive traits in some of his favorite professional athletes, he has created this broad list:

- Hard-Working
- Goal-Driven
- Dependable
- Innovative
- Studious
- Self-Sufficient
- Competitive
- Independent
- Introspective

Jesse's list includes nine values that are important to him. He believes that living these values will help him create the best version of himself and define how others perceive him. This is the exciting part of building a brand: you can *craft* how your customers see you if you're willing to put in the work.

SHARPEN YOUR VALUES

It's far easier to be great at five skills than fifteen. Similarly, living up to a long list of values, such as the one Jesse created, may be difficult. If he hangs the list inside his locker, how can he possibly work on living up to all the values at once? He may end up being good at living some values, but not really great at any of them. Narrowing your list down to three or four "core" values allows you to define what you stand for more clearly.

Let's review Jesse's list. You may notice patterns or themes that allow us to combine some of the values. For example, the values of Hard-Working and Dependable have some similarities. Both speak to showing up consistently to put in the work. They speak about the amount of effort Jesse will put in and how he can work alongside his team. Let's combine these values into something actionable:

Dependable Hard-Worker

This is something Jesse can *be*. He can strive to present himself as a dependable hard worker to his coach, teammates, and even people off the field. Jesse can be a dependable hard worker at work, in the classroom, and even with his family. It's an image Jesse can show to the world around him. Even more importantly, this aspect of his personal brand can set him apart from other people. And the best part? It comes from values Jesse believes in and is already living.

Here are some other combinations that make Jesse's values actionable:

Studious Innovator (Combines Studious and Innovative)

Goal-Driven Competitor (Combines Goal-driven and Competitive)

Independent Thinker (Combines Independent and Introspective)

This list of four attributes is much clearer. You may notice "self-sufficient" has fallen off the list. And that's okay. Jesse recognized self-sufficiency as an integral part of the other core values he lists above, and is therefore too broad to include on his list. Similarly, as you narrow down your list, you may find a trait that overlaps with your values. Think about what makes your core values specific and actionable.

Jesse now has a smaller list he can put into action. Think about how customers from sports, school, and life would perceive his brand based on these values. Jesse believes these four core values present the best version of him. Now he can set a goal to live up to these values and work hard to achieve them. And, just like that 'Torpedo Bat', Jesse's customers will be ready to buy the unique product in front of them.

THE FINAL SCORE

In this chapter, we discussed how products must set themselves apart in a competitive market. A customer can choose between one hundred different baseball bats. *Why* would they choose your specific bat?

Imagine yourself as a product, just like the baseball bat, and think about what sets you apart from others. The great news is that you are exceptionally unique. No one else can recreate the blend of things that make up *you*, which means you have elements that stand out. It's time to identify these strengths and aspirations and use them to your advantage.

Your *values* (what you stand for) will help drive your brand (how you are perceived by your customers). We walked you through an example of identifying an athlete's values and determining how they might resonate with different customers. Then we narrowed the list down to four core values that represented the best version of the athlete he wanted to present.

So now that we've said what our values are, we're done, right? No, of course not. You didn't think it would be that easy, did you? Your customers will always make assumptions about you. Those assumptions aren't based on what you tell them. Customers define your attributes based on what you do. In other words, it is not enough to say, "I'm a goal-driven competitor." Now it's time to do the work.

CHAPTER 3 EXERCISE

1. **Identify your current values.** Review the list of values from this chapter and the back of the book (Appendix A). Write down 8-10 values you connect with. These can be values you already have or ones you hope to have in the future.

1.	6.
2.	7.
3.	8.
4.	9.
5.	10.

2. **Remember your customers.** Return to the list of customers we created in Chapter 2. Which customers did you prioritize? How do the values you created speak to these customers?

    a. First Customer: _____

b. How do the values above speak to this customer?

_____

_____

_____

_____

_____

_____

c. Second Customer:_____

d. How do the values above speak to this customer?

_____

_____

_____

_____

_____

_____

3. **Sharpen your list.** Review your list of 8-10 values and choose your top 3-5 values. You might be able to combine two values into one stronger choice. Finalize your actionable values for your personal brand.

TOP VALUES
1.
2.
3.
4.
5.

4. **Reflect on your brand.** Read your top values and think about the brand you are promoting. Remember, you are a product. Is this the best version of you? Is this the person you want to promote to your customers? *Why?*

_____

_____

_____

_____

_____

_____

BUILD YOUR ACTION PLAN

THE ATHLETE'S JOURNEY

Serena Williams is one of the most successful players in tennis history. She physically dominated opponents on the court on her way to 23 Grand Slam singles titles, four Olympic gold medals, and countless other awards. She is the world's only player (male or female) to achieve the Career Golden Slam in singles and doubles, meaning she has won all four of the major championships, and Olympic Gold as a singles *and* doubles player[1]. Many tennis experts, fans, and sports analysts consider her the greatest female tennis player of all time.

Of course, this success didn't happen by accident. No, Williams planned it.

Serena Williams knew the average women's tennis match lasted under two hours. But instead of training her body to endure two hours of intense competition, she doubled it. Williams developed a training plan to play "all out" for four hours, giving her a significant competitive edge[2]. When opponents would tire toward the end of the match, Williams was just reaching the midway point of her training regimen. She identified being physically dominant as an important value and created a plan to achieve that result.

Williams trained on the court for four hours daily in addition to strength and cardiovascular exercise. She followed a routine and was disciplined with her time. Following this plan allowed her to become stronger and last longer than virtually any other opponent.

As you can see, the greatest female tennis player of all time didn't simply say, "I will outlast my opponents" and hope it would happen. She devised a plan for success and followed it until her goal came true. This is the next step in our journey to developing our best selves. We must take the values we believe in and create an action plan to bring these values to life.

It's time to build your Brand Action Plan.

WHAT IS AN ACTION PLAN?

In the previous chapter, you created a list of values that are important to you and your customers. But now that you have these values, you may be wondering what you can do with them. Hanging them inside your locker might be a good start, but we all know that goals aren't reached by accident. For most of us, we need to take specific steps to achieve the goals we set.

An action plan will help you turn your aspirations into reality. Just like a coach presents a game plan to the team before they leave the locker room, your personal action plan will provide you with steps aimed at helping you win. So, how do we do this? By brainstorming daily, weekly, and monthly steps that drive the values you identified as being important to you.

The Brand Action Plan is a series of steps you can take every day, every week, and every month to create the best version of YOU in sports, school, and life.

PUT IT INTO ACTION

To demonstrate this concept, let's return to our lacrosse player, Jesse, and the list of actionable values he created:

Dependable Hard Worker
Studious Innovator
Goal-Driven Competitor
Independent Thinker

Let's start with his first one: *Dependable Hard Worker*. What can Jesse do to live up to this value? Remember, you can't simply say you are a dependable hard worker and expect your customers to believe it. Think back to our definition of a brand in Chapter 1. Your customers will know you are a dependable hard worker based on the "intangible sum" of their interactions with you. That means Jesse's actions must reflect this value until he is *recognized* as a dependable hard worker by his classmates, coaches, and other important customers in his life.

To live out this value, Jesse can put daily, weekly, and monthly actions in place. Check out the example below:

Value: *Dependable Hard Worker*

Every Day:

1. Give 100% effort at practice and in class every day.
2. Show up on time (or early), ready to work.
3. Complete all assignments and training on time.
4. Participate in class discussions once a day and ask questions when I don't understand something.
5. Help set up and break down equipment for practices each day.

Every Week:

1. Volunteer at a charity cause for an hour a week.
2. At the start of every week, I plan my homework and study sessions to stay ahead in class.
3. Spend an extra 20 minutes in the gym once a week.

Every Month:

1. Set aside one hour a month to review video footage of practices or study professional lacrosse players online to improve my skills.
2. Complete one extra credit assignment in one of my classes once a month.
3. Take initiative to lead a group or team project.

There's no hard rule for the number of steps for each category. Aim for three to five daily steps, three weekly steps, and at least one monthly step. You may find more steps for your particular brand values, and that's okay.

What do you think of the action plan Jesse has created? Can you see how the daily goals relate to the weekly goals, which then relate to the monthly goals? All these steps should relate to one another, as they are designed to bring Jesse closer to his larger goal: showing the people around him that he is a dependable and hard worker. Now fast-forward six months. If Jesse commits to the plan he created for himself, how do you think his customers will perceive him?

Don't forget, Jesse has three more actionable values he established: *Studious Innovator, Goal-Driven Competitor, and Independent Thinker.* Now he must go through the same exercise and identify steps he can take every day, every week, and every month for each of those values. Once he chooses steps for all of his values, he will have a complete Brand Action Plan.

If Jesse can follow this plan for the next few months, he will be living the best version of himself and influencing how those around him (his customers) view him.

JESSE'S BRAND ACTION PLAN

Value: Dependable Hard Worker	
Daily Actions	1. Give 100% effort at practice and in class every day. 2. Show up on time (or early), ready to work. 3. Complete all assignments and training on time. 4. Participate in class discussions once a day and ask questions when I don't understand something. 5. Help set up and break down equipment for practices each day.
Weekly Actions	1. Volunteer at a charity cause for an hour a week. 2. At the start of every week, I plan my homework and study sessions to stay ahead in class.

	3. Spend an extra 15 minutes in the gym once a week.
Monthly Actions	1. Set aside one hour a month to review video footage of practices or study professional lacrosse players online to improve my skills. 2. Complete one extra credit assignment in one of my classes once a month. 3. Take initiative to lead a group or team project.

Value: Studious Innovator	
Daily Actions	1. Read (beyond mainstream noise). 2. Be curious. Ask *why* we do certain things in practice or the classroom to gain a deeper understanding. Think about how we can do things differently. 3. Carve out dedicated, non-negotiable time for school work.
Weekly Actions	1. Listen to a podcast about a topic in my field.

	2. Read one article about an industry trend.
Monthly Actions	1. Start a blog and write something once a month.
	2. Create an Innovation Challenge and find a process, play, or piece of equipment to improve.
	3. Work on a group project/activity on a topic outside of my comfort zone to spark creativity and learn something new.

Value: Goal-Driven Competitor	
Daily Actions	1. Set 1-3 priorities for the day, and reflect at the end of each day on whether I achieved them.
	2. Stay disciplined with my routines of sleep, training, studying, and nutrition.
	3. Spend 3-5 minutes visualizing winning, improving, or overcoming an obstacle.
Weekly Actions	1. Use data to benchmark my progress in strength, speed, assists, and turnovers.

	2. Share progress with teammates and encourage them to do the same.
	3. "Reward" myself with a night off for a week of good grades on homework and tests.
Monthly Actions	1. Ask for feedback from a teacher or coach about a specific skill I am trying to improve.
	2. Watch film on role model athletes to study their technique.
	3. Conduct a personal performance review to see which goals I am hitting and where I may need more focus.

Value: Independent Thinker	
Daily Actions	1. Read.
	2. Be self-reliant for my academic and practice responsibilities.
	3. Don't rely on others for tasks I know I can do myself.
Weekly Actions	1. Make at least one independent judgment. Ask myself, "Would I still believe this if no one else did?"

	2. Be introspective. Ask myself, "Why do I believe this? Why do I feel this way? Why did I react this way?"
Monthly Actions	1. Write a blog or article about something I feel passionate about. 2. Speak with someone who has an opposing view on a particular topic.

You may have noticed that a few of the actions above are repeated for two different values. This is okay. In fact, it only helps you! We all love to be efficient when it comes to training, schoolwork, and life. If the same action can serve two different values, then go ahead and use it for both.

Now let's think back to Serena Williams' plan to be the most physically dominant player in tennis. She followed specific steps to achieve that identity. But Williams didn't just dominate on the tennis court. She also became a fashion icon with her own clothing and jewelry lines, a philanthropist and advocate for underrepresented groups, and even a movie producer. Each of these accomplishments is based on what Williams values. To reach these goals, she needed to put a plan into place for *each* value that was important to her brand. Over time, we've come to recognize Williams as a force in tennis, fashion, philanthropy, and media, not because she tells us she is, but because of her consistent behaviors in each of those areas over time.

By the way, I practice what I preach. If you're interested in another example of an action plan, flip to Appendix B to see *my own* Brand Action Plan. You may find this helpful as you start to imagine your life beyond just sports. (Go there to see why playing Scrabble every day is an intentional part of my plan!)

JUDGE YOUR SUCCESS

So, how do you know when your action plan has succeeded? The first answer might sound a bit cliché, but it's the truth. You ask yourself: *How do I feel?*

The list of values you created includes traits that are important to you and your customers. If you've spent a month following your action plan, ask yourself if you're living and embodying the values you aspire to. After a month of following his daily, weekly, and monthly steps, Jesse should feel like a dependable hard worker, studious innovator, goal-driven competitor, and independent thinker. If he doesn't feel this way, then he may want to adjust the steps in his action plan. Similarly, if Jesse couldn't complete his action plan this month, his steps may have been too ambitious or unrealistic. The important thing is to find a plan that is manageable yet still challenging, and ultimately makes you feel like you're living out your values.

Once you've found a plan that makes *you* feel closer to the traits you are aspiring to, it's time to look outside of yourself. Remember that we are building your brand. This means we need to know how customers perceive you. Listen carefully to things your coaches or teachers say about you, either in person or through written assignments. Does the feedback align with the values you're striving for? Lock in to their actions as well. Are they calling on you in class more? Is your coach giving you a spot in the starting lineup or using you as an example in practice? How are teammates responding to the changes they see in your behavior?

Finally, there's no harm in asking! Of course, you won't walk up to your coach and ask, "Am I a dependable hard worker?" But there are other ways to ask this question. You might tell your coach that you've been going to the gym every morning and ask if he's noticed any differences. You could tell your teacher that you've been working hard to prioritize your schoolwork and ask if there's anything else you can do to succeed in the class. These questions serve two purposes: One, they allow you to give your customers a taste of your brand and point out what makes you unique compared to others. Second, these questions give you real-time feedback on what your customers want. Knowing exactly what your customers are looking for is invaluable information as you hone and perfect your action plan.

MAKE IT SUSTAINABLE

Think of your action plan like a basketball player's free-throw practice-it's not just for the beginning of the season. Players consistently take reps during every practice, and on their own time, both in-season and off-season. Consistent effort over time is key to mastering this skill. Similarly, we should view our action plan as an ongoing process, not a one-month project.

Every few months, take a moment to reflect on your values and plan. How are the steps working for you? Do you notice a change in yourself or in the way others interact with you? Are you able to commit to your daily, weekly, and monthly actions, or are you having trouble keeping up? Answering these questions will help you decide whether to adjust your action plan for the next few months. Remember, this is a long-term process that doesn't happen overnight.

The good news is you are built for this. As a student-athlete, you are almost always in training. You work out. You study film, or you study your playbook. You also study for class. Building your personal brand is just another piece of training integrated into what you're already doing.

Finally, there is one more point to consider. Just as there are threats to your success in competition, we're about to discover that there are threats to your brand as well.

THE FINAL SCORE

In this chapter, we discussed your action plan. The Brand Action Plan is a series of steps you can enact on a daily, weekly, and monthly basis to ensure your customers see what you want them to see.

We gave an example of an action plan for one value an athlete wants to embody. Using our athlete example from the previous chapter, we discussed Jesse's monthly, weekly, and daily steps to becoming a *Dependable Hard Worker*. Then, we built out steps for all of Jesse's values. These action steps are things Jesse can follow over the next few months (and even years) to build his brand and create a product that appeals to his customers.

But how do we judge the success of this action plan? First, we check in with ourselves to see if we feel like the living embodiment of our values. Second, we become keen observers and listeners to our customers. We key in to what coaches, teachers, and family say about us and how they act around us. We can also ask them direct questions about our goals or our actions to gather even more helpful information about what our customers are looking for.

By creating our Brand Action Plan, we can live out the values we define as the best version of ourselves, thereby creating a very clear and unique brand that people will be eager to buy.

CHAPTER 4 EXERCISE

1. **Review your actionable values.** Review your list of 3-5 actionable values you established in the last chapter. Do they still feel relevant and important to you? Make sure you feel great about these values, since we are building your action plan (and your brand) around them. Write down your top values.

TOP VALUES
1.
2.
3.
4.
5.

2. **Build your Brand Action Plan.** Write down one value in each box with daily, weekly, and monthly steps you can take to become the person you aspire to be. There are five templates below. Choose 3 to 5 values that speak to you.

Remember, this is your plan to succeed in sports, school, and life. Take your time and be thoughtful. This won't be easy, but it's the most important step to becoming the best version of you.

Brand Value:	
Daily Actions	1. 2. 3.
Weekly Actions	1.

	2.
	3.
Monthly Actions	1.
	2.
	3.

Brand Value:	
Daily Actions	1. 2. 3.
Weekly Actions	1. 2. 3.

Monthly Actions	1.
	2.
	3.

Brand Value:

Daily Actions	1.
	2.
	3.

Weekly Actions	1.
	2.
	3.
Monthly Actions	1.
	2.
	3.

Brand Value:	
Daily Actions	1. 2. 3.
Weekly Actions	1. 2. 3.

Monthly Actions	1.
	2.
	3.

Brand Value:	
Daily Actions	1.
	2.
	3.

Weekly Actions	1.
	2.
	3.
Monthly Actions	1.
	2.
	3.

Note: There are additional blank templates in Appendix C.

YOUR DIGITAL BRAND

THE ATHLETE'S JOURNEY

Amir Khan would likely never be mistaken for an elite athlete. He's not big or fast. He doesn't possess any impressive athletic skills. He simply loves basketball. So when Khan arrived at McNeese State University in Louisiana, he jumped at the chance to volunteer as student manager for the men's basketball team.

Student Manager is an unglamorous job. Khan cleaned the locker room, did laundry, and performed other menial tasks to help the team prepare for competition. But the Sports Management major embraced his role in every way. "If they kept manager stats for [shooting drill] rebounding and wiping up wet spots on the court, I'd put up Wilt Chamberlain numbers," he said[1]. Simply put, Khan loved the McNeese State Cowboys and their players.

One day, just before a big game, Khan hyped up his team by rapping a song while wearing an enormous boom box around his neck. Khan nailed the rap ("In & Out" by Lud Foe) word-for-word as he led the march from the locker room to the court. Khan's enthusiasm was nothing new to the players who saw his enthusiasm in practice every day. But when a teammate recorded Khan's performance and shared it through social media, he became an overnight viral sensation[1].

Khan earned the nickname "Aura" for his energy and love for the team. He began to share more videos of his pre-game hype sessions. When McNeese State upset Clemson in the first round of the 2025 NCAA Men's Basketball Tournament (their first tourney win in program history), Khan's aura took off.

McNeese cheerleaders began wearing Aura socks with Khan's face emblazoned on the side. Businesses jumped on the social media frenzy, signing Khan to name, image, and likeness (NIL) deals worth more than six figures[2]. The social media attention helped Khan sign a deal with Topps for his own trading card.

Khan could never have envisioned this level of popularity and success when he agreed to be a student manager. A viral video changed his world in an instant. But his journey offers important lessons on how social media can elevate your brand to larger audiences, and what you need to think about to prepare.

THE VAST SEA OF SOCIAL MEDIA

Social media usage has exploded in recent years because of its ability to connect people. Think of any topic, interest, or hobby. Chances are, you can find others who share the same passion through social media. Platforms have helped launch a generation of influencers and celebrities who can reach audiences like never before. With the influx of social media in our society, we cannot ignore the benefits (and possible pitfalls) of social media when it comes to our personal brands.

With new platforms constantly emerging and others fading away, it's nearly impossible to count them all. But the most widely used sites tend to serve distinct purposes. It's worth considering each platform as you develop your online presence. How can you see social media as a tool to help you build your brand?

Let's look at some of the most popular sites and what they're generally used for:

General social networking: Instagram, TikTok, Twitter/X, Facebook
Messaging: WhatsApp, Messenger, WeChat, Telegram, Discord
Gaming: Twitch, GameTree
Video/Photo Sharing: YouTube, TikTok, SnapChat, Instagram, Pinterest
Online Communities: Reddit, Discord, Quora
Professional Networking: LinkedIn

You may already be active on one or more of these platforms, but have you ever thought of how your feed, messages, or photos are influencing your brand? Take the time to look at your profiles through the lens of your personal brand.

THE DIGITAL YOU

Social media plays a crucial role in personal branding by offering a platform to showcase your personality, connect with audiences, and build a strong online presence. More views and followers can mean more growth for your brand. But jumping into the virtual world can be tricky or even uncomfortable. It's not easy to know what to post, how much to share, or how often. Fortunately, you already have a playbook to help guide you.

First, let's start with your customers. Remember those marketing teams that created their ideal customer for their product? They understood their customer demographics, including knowing which social media platforms potential customers are most likely to use. Connecting with teammates lends itself to Instagram or one of the messaging apps. But if you're trying to build a fan following, you might also consider posting videos on YouTube or TikTok. Always start with your customers, just like companies do when they market their product.

Once you've chosen the most important customers, go back to the brand values you created in Chapters 3 and 4. These are the values that you determined represent the best version of yourself– the version you want your customers to see. So why not use that as the foundation for your social media activity?

If being a *Good Teammate* is important to you, check in on teammates through social media. Post photos of team activities. Support your teammates with positive comments on their posts. Maybe *Fashion-Conscious* is an important part of who you are. Share articles and pictures of the latest fashion trends. Create your own videos commenting on the latest styles. If *Environmentalism* is something you feel deeply about, use social media to raise awareness about a clean-up project. If *Leadership* is a core value, use social media to organize additional practices or film study, and find blogs about leadership development. There are endless examples.

Remembering that your digital presence is simply an extension of who you already are is really important. Think back to our viral hero, Amir "Aura" Khan. One reason his brand took off so quickly was because it was authentic. Khan was genuinely enthusiastic about his role as Student Manager, regardless of whether he was being recorded. He didn't pretend to be someone else to become famous. He stayed true to what he valued.

Take a look at the pictures you've posted and ask yourself: Who is this person? What do these photos and captions say about their brand? Make sure your digital presence accurately reflects the best version of yourself that you are striving to build and maintain.

AVOID THE TRAPS

You might feel this is all a bit too calculated. Maybe you're thinking, *Social media should be spontaneous and fun, not planned and pre-determined.* To some degree, you're right. Social media *is* fun, and it can be a great way to connect with others who share your interests. But as a student-athlete trying to build the best version of yourself for your customers, you need to think differently about your social media profiles.

First, virtually anything you post on social media lives on indefinitely. That trash-talking comment you made on a competitor's page last year may come back to haunt you the next time you play. A post that may seem clever or witty today may seem offensive or ignorant in the future. Future employers, coaches, and teammates often search social media, sometimes even before they've met you in person. What brand do you want them to see? And will the posts you make today age well with your future customers?

Second, social media's ability to reach large audiences is one of its greatest appeals. It also happens to be one of its greatest risks. If someone tags you in a photo showing poor judgment or questionable behavior, you may find it difficult to overcome the negative reactions to that photo. (Remember the photo of Michael Phelps smoking pot at a party?) Once a negative perception about you grows on social media, the viral ability to spread makes it very difficult to regain the narrative and protect your brand.

Lastly, it's much easier to say or do something questionable when we don't have to face the immediate negative consequences. That's why you see so many people, athletes, and fans post horrific (and sometimes abusive) comments about others that they wouldn't dare say to the person directly. Hiding behind a keyboard or touchscreen is no excuse to contradict the values you've set for yourself, and even anonymous posts can sometimes be traced back to their source.

Developing your online presence can still be a lot of fun. Just remember to pause before you hit post and think about how your customers might react.

MAKE IT WORK FOR YOU

As your personal brand grows, so will your following on social media. College athletes, like Caitlin Clark and Angel Reese, were catapulted into stardom as they gained success in the world of women's basketball, gaining thousands of new social media followers with each big step in their careers. Both of these female athletes leveraged their social media to connect with their fans, posting about basketball, responding to comments, and sharing personal stories[3]. You may not reach their level of fame, but the lessons still apply. They are using social media to promote their brand to great effect.

So what happens when you want to share a goofy video of yourself with your family that doesn't line up with your brand? Or maybe you'd like to comment on a friend's post without the whole world seeing that reaction. You have another option: multiple accounts. Many professional athletes, celebrities, and even high-powered business executives will keep a private account that is only for friends and family. The other account is for their public image. This is a very intentional way to use social media as a tool for your brand.

Others choose to have little to no digital footprint, though this is less common. At points in your career, you may find that social media isn't serving your values. You might decide that social media is a distraction, contributing negatively to your mental health and serving as a roadblock to building the best version of you. If posting on social media starts to matter more than getting to the gym, showing up to practice, and engaging with your teammates, then it's actually hurting your brand, not helping it.

The important thing is to be aware of social media and how it *could* be used. It's up to you to choose how you use these platforms. With a bit of awareness, you can speak directly to your customers and get a significant leg up in presenting a careful image of your brand.

THE FINAL SCORE

In this chapter, we discussed the prevalence of social media and its impact on your brand. Social media can be a very positive influence, allowing you to speak directly to your customers and reach new ones you could never meet in life. Thinking about your customers can also influence which social media platforms you use to maximize your reach.

We then discussed how your social media presence can (and should) reflect your *values*. Just as you work to make your customers see a specific version of you in the real world, you need to do the same on social media. Make sure the images you post, comments you make, and content you share strengthen the brand you are creating rather than hinder it.

Pay attention to the pitfalls of social media as well. Social media is forever, which means something you post today could come back to hurt your brand in the future. It is also *public*. One post can be seen by many people and shared by others instantly. Ask yourself: Am I okay with this post being seen by the world? If the answer is *no*, then perhaps you need some private accounts that will allow you to share things in a safer (less public) environment. Finally, it's easier to say things when hiding behind a screen. Don't let that false sense of safety fool you. Say things online that you would say in person, and make sure those words align with your personal brand values.

Now that we've discussed how to build your brand, it's time to talk about the next step: how to protect it. Any athlete knows that muscles will disappear if you don't continue to use them. You must maintain what you've built, but you also must adapt to change if you want to keep your brand relevant to your customers.

CHAPTER 5 EXERCISE

1. **List all of your social media accounts.** How often do you post on each one, and for what purpose?

Social Media Account	How Often Do You Post?	What's the Primary Purpose of This Account?

2. **Look at the last five photos you've posted on social media.** What assumptions could your customers make about your brand based on those photos alone?

_____

_____

_____

_____

_____

3. **Look back at some of your earliest posts on social media.** Do you feel differently about them today? Are there any posts you regret making? If so, why?

_____

_____

_____

_____

_____

_____

PART THREE:

PROTECT THE BRAND

"The knowledge that everything good can be taken away at any second is what makes me work so hard."

—Ronda Rousey

Mixed martial artist, first female UFC Champion, Olympic bronze medalist

BRANDS CHANGE

THE ATHLETE'S JOURNEY

Lance Armstrong was a competitive cyclist and elite athlete who won the sport's most prestigious race, the Tour De France, a record-shattering seven consecutive years[1]. This grueling competition lasts three weeks and spans over 2,000 miles across France. Armstrong climbed the cycling mountain, both figuratively and literally. But along the way, his brand took as many turns as the roads he biked, starting with him nearly dying before his first Tour victory.

In 1996, Armstrong was diagnosed with Stage 3 cancer[1]. Many doctors didn't think he would live, let alone cycle again. But Armstrong went through rounds of chemotherapy and surgery to beat the odds. Remarkably, Armstrong showed up at his team's training camp in France a few months later. In February of 1997, he was declared cancer-free.

Armstrong's cancer diagnosis and recovery changed his brand forever. This little-known athlete, near death, survived cancer and was now working himself back to the top of his game. He became a symbol of perseverance and hope. He could have ignored this change to focus on training alone. Instead, Armstrong saw this change as an opportunity to set a new goal for himself: to help others with cancer.

In 1997, Armstrong founded the Lance Armstrong Foundation for other survivors and caregivers. The organization held charity bike races and raised money for support services and cancer research. Then, in 1998, Armstrong won his first Tour de France and became one of the most recognizable athletes in the world. He was tough and resilient. He was a survivor, the founder of a life-changing cancer foundation, and now a champion.

Then it all came crashing down.

In 2004, a book raised questions about whether Armstrong had used performance-enhancing drugs[2]. Since his drug tests had always come back clean, few wanted to believe that this icon, who championed healthy living, would ever resort to doping. Armstrong himself denied the allegations. But the rumors persisted, and new allegations continued to surface. The United States Anti-Doping Agency accused Armstrong of doping and even trafficking drugs[3]. Finally, in a 2013 interview, Armstrong admitted to doping[4].

Athlete. Survivor. Inspiration. Champion. Liar. Cheater.

All of Armstrong's sponsors dropped him[5]. Nike even cut ties to Armstrong's charity, the Lance Armstrong Foundation, which has since been renamed Livestrong[6]. The Tour de France stripped Armstrong of all his titles[5], completing one of the most significant falls from grace in the world of sports. Once again, Armstrong's brand had changed forever.

Much of Armstrong's success and demise was self-driven, but the lesson remains: brands change over time. There is no finish line for building the best version of yourself, only twists and turns like the races Armstrong competed in. What's important is to recognize that change *will* happen. The more prepared you are for change, the better you'll be able to respond.

RECOGNIZE CHANGE

Think of the anecdote of boiling a frog. As the story goes, if you throw a frog in a pot of boiling water, it will immediately jump out. But if you throw a frog in a pot of cold water and slowly raise the temperature, the frog will stay in the pot until it is boiled alive.

This is a story about change. It's easy to notice the boiling water. That's a big change that shocks the frog into taking action. But raising the temperature over a long period of time is a slow change that often goes unnoticed. You might think you'll be able to see the warning signs that affect your brand and stop the change before any negative ramifications occur. But change doesn't always happen quickly. If you're not careful, your brand can erode over time, so slowly that you don't realize it.

The first step to maintaining your brand is to be acutely aware of changes. Changes to yourself, your customers, and the environment around you. If you're not paying attention, your brand could end up like the frog... cooked.

We often see this trend in business with companies or products that didn't react to change. Kodak, an iconic American brand known for photography and film, famously miscalculated the impact of digital technology and went bankrupt[7]. Toys R Us was *the* place to buy children's toys from the 1960s to the 1990s, with aisles of games, action figures, and stuffed animals. But by 2018, after decades of big box stores and online retailers capturing market share, the one-time wonderland for kids had closed all of its stores[8]. Blockbuster dominated the market for movie rentals. As mailing and streaming services grew, Blockbuster failed to recognize the threat to its business until it was too late[9]. These companies were built on technology, fun, and innovation, but they were later perceived as outdated, boring, and obsolete. Their brands faded into something unrecognizable because these companies failed to keep up with a constantly changing world.

STAY ALERT

Just as company reputations can change over time, your brand can also erode into something you don't recognize. Think of people in your own life. Perhaps you had a teammate who used to be an unselfish player, but with a school record in reach, they are now more concerned about personal stats. Maybe a teacher was very helpful at the beginning of the school year, but now expects students to be more self-sufficient. There are many reasons personal brands can change. In the next chapter, we'll discuss some of these reasons, including things you have control over and things you do not. But regardless of *why* your brand changes, you must become an expert at recognizing signs of change.

Let's say one of your values is to be *Innovative*. This word inherently requires you to be up to speed on the latest trends in your field so you can reinvent and try new things. But if you're not putting in this work, you can quickly go from someone innovative to someone outdated. The expert can become incompetent or out of touch. The collaborator can become isolated and one-sided. Ultimately, your very valuable brand can become something you don't intend it to be.

We can see more examples in the following chart. The column on the left represents brand values you may identify with. But if you fail to maintain your daily, weekly, and monthly actions, others may perceive your brand by the characteristics in the column on the right.

Trustworthy	→	Doubtful
Exciting	→	Uninspiring
Helpful	→	Frustrating
Expert	→	Inept
Delightful	→	Disappointing
Friendly	→	Rude
Unique	→	Common

When we step back and view the big picture, it's not hard to see how your brand can erode over time. Remember our lacrosse player, Jesse, from Chapters 3 and 4? He had an action plan to drive his value of being a dependable hard worker. What happens if he stops following the plan? One day, he sleeps in too late and shows up late to practice. The next week, he decides to skip his volunteer hours. And maybe a few days later, he chooses to go to a party instead of reviewing the film of his last game. If these small behaviors continue week after week, Jesse's customers will begin to see him as unreliable and uncommitted.

If Jesse doesn't care enough to maintain the habits driving his brand, why should his customers care?

IMMEDIATE CHANGE

A "slow boil" isn't the only threat to your brand. While it's important to recognize changes that can impact your brand over time, it's also important to be aware of situations that can impact your brand instantly.

In 2016, Colin Kaepernick took a knee during the national anthem, and his brand changed in an instant.

Kaepernick spent six seasons in the National Football League as a quarterback for the San Francisco 49ers[10]. In the wave of police shootings and the Black Lives Matter movement, Kaepernick chose to protest police brutality in the United States by kneeling during the ceremonial playing of the United States National Anthem, which occurs at the beginning of every NFL game. Kaepernick was thrown into the spotlight, the subject of news stories across the country and around the world.

Some people applauded Kaepernick for his actions. Others denounced his protest as disrespectful to the American flag and what it stands for. What is irrefutable is that Kaepernick's brand changed forever. He became a symbol for something much larger than himself.

Perhaps you know some people in your life who have been catapulted into change instantly. It may have even happened to you. A talented teammate gets recruited to play for a prominent club, immediately changing your team dynamic. Maybe you had to switch teams mid-season because a parent changed jobs and moved your family to a new city. Many student athletes were quickly affected by the COVID-19 pandemic, the required quarantines, and the sudden changes in college eligibility.

So, how do we manage significant change when it happens instantly? What can we do if we suddenly find ourselves faced with a significant change to our brand? Well, we think about our values and the customers who are most important to us. It's impossible to know whether Kaepernick *knew* that taking a knee would impact him for the rest of his life. We don't know if he thought about how this would change his brand. But once his brand was affected, Kaepernick adapted. He returned to his values and decided that issues of social justice and equality were important to him. He picked which customers he wanted to speak to, and he doubled down on these values.

Kaepernick didn't change his mind. He recognized his decision would be unpopular with many people, but he stood his ground and stuck with his values. It's no different for your own personal brand. If change arrives unexpectedly, you'll have to decide which customers are most important to you. What are the values you want to stand behind that speak to those customers?

THE FINAL SCORE

In this chapter, we established that brands can change if we are not paying attention. Sometimes the brand can slowly erode over a long period of time. Sometimes it can change in an instant. It's important to regularly evaluate yourself, your customers, and your environment to ensure your brand continues to align with the best version of yourself.

We've seen companies transform from innovative to obsolete. Similarly, your brand can change over time if you're not paying attention. One missed school assignment might seem insignificant, but what if this is the beginning of a pattern? A few missed assignments over time would redefine your brand.

You also need to be prepared for your brand to change in an instant. If you are suddenly faced with this, it's time for you to decide how you will respond. Return to the customers that are important to you and the values you've set for yourself. What are you going to stand for?

Now that we understand how brands can change, it's time to dig into *why* they change. Global pandemics, sidelining injuries, coaches' decisions, and NCAA regulations may feel out of your control. But here's a little secret: most of the reasons brands change are actually controlled by...

YOU.

CHAPTER 6 EXERCISE

1. **Think of an athlete or famous individual you used to like but feel very differently about now.**

   a. Athlete: _____

   b. Why did your opinion of them change?

   _____

   _____

   _____

   _____

   _____

   _____

   c. Was this a fast change, or did your opinion of them change slowly over time?

   _____

   _____

   _____

   _____

   _____

   _____

2. **Imagine a situation that could change your brand in an instant, either positively or negatively.** Describe the situation and how you would react.

   a. Describe the situation:

   _____

   _____

   _____

   _____

   _____

   _____

   b. How will you react to the situation?

   _____

   _____

   _____

   _____

   _____

   _____

3. **Choose one of your values.** How might that value erode over time, and what can you do to prevent that change?

   a. Value: _____

   b. How could this value erode over time?

   _____

   _____

   _____

   _____

   _____

   _____

   c. What can you do to prevent that change?

   _____

   _____

   _____

   _____

   _____

   _____

WHAT YOU CONTROL

THE ATHLETE'S JOURNEY

For many athletes, the Olympic Games are the crowning achievement of their careers. The opportunity to represent their country is the highest honor they can achieve, a goal they have relentlessly driven toward for years. Many athletes dream of the moment when they will stand on the podium with a medal around their neck, hearing their country's national anthem echoing throughout the stadium. It's a once-in-a-lifetime opportunity that depends just as much on the athlete's dedication and skill as it does on *time*. After all, the Olympics occur only once every four years per sport and must coincide with when athletes reach their peak performance.

1980 was a summer Olympic year. U.S. athletes in swimming, rowing, gymnastics, basketball, and many other sports set their sights on the summer games. They trained hard, some for their whole lives, and beat out their competition at their sport's Olympic trials to earn the honor of representing their country. Four hundred and sixty-six U.S. athletes were set to compete on the world's biggest stage[1]. And then, through no fault of their own, that dream was stripped away from them.

In 1980, the International Olympic Committee awarded the Olympic Games to Moscow, Soviet Union (present-day Russia). The Soviet Union was our largest political and economic rival, and our countries were engaged in a decades-long cold war. Tensions between the two countries ramped up in 1979 when the Soviets invaded Afghanistan to support a communist regime. Despite the Olympic theme of unity through sport, sending our athletes to our largest rival during a time of significant political tension seemed unwise. President Jimmy Carter decided to boycott the Moscow Olympics, and the United States Olympic Committee supported this decision, leaving athletes with no say in the matter[2]. All of their training, hard work, and sacrifice was for nothing. Their chance to be forever known as an "Olympic Athlete" was dashed by a decision they couldn't control.

What did the athletes do next? Each responded in their own way. Some younger athletes knew they would still be in their physical prime in another four years and continued training to qualify for the next Olympics. Some older athletes knew these Olympic Games were their last shot at a medal and moved on to other careers. Many focused on other international competitions. Ten days after the Olympics, swimmer Craig Beardsley set a world record in the 200M butterfly with a time a second and a half faster than the Soviet swimmer who had just won the 1980 Olympic gold medal[1].

These athletes had to determine how to respond when they were directly impacted by a significant change. It's important to remember that no matter how careful you are with your brand, and no matter how purposeful you are with your brand action plan, sometimes there are forces outside of your control. What can you do when you've done everything *right* to promote and hone your brand, but things still go wrong?

WHY BRANDS CHANGE

Change is inevitable. As we learned in the previous chapter, the only way to keep your brand relevant, strong, and working for you is to be aware of change so you can respond before it's too late. While it's impossible to predict every scenario that could lead to change, you could probably brainstorm an entire page of factors that would impact your brand. Here are a few of the things you might write down:

Social media posts on your personal account.

Training sessions in the gym.

The starting lineup (and whether or not you are on it).

An injury.

Effort level in the classroom.

Your team's performance.

Each of these factors has the potential to help or hurt your brand. For example, one social media post could result in thousands of new followers, while another may cost you a job. Or your team's success could lead to more scouts at your game, but if your team is struggling, you may not get noticed. It isn't hard to imagine the positive and negative sides of nearly every example. But pay close attention to factors that can impact your brand, and you'll notice an interesting pattern.

The reasons brands change over time fall neatly into two categories: Things you can't control, and things you can.

Take the starting lineup. No matter how hard you train or how much you prove yourself, the coach has the ultimate decision over whether or not you start the game. The coach may base his or her decision on several factors, including who you are playing against, the opponent's strengths and weaknesses, or how well one of your teammates in the same position happens to be playing at the time. Just as the athletes of the 1980 Olympics had no choice over whether they would compete, you will face *external* factors you cannot control.

Other changes are a direct result of your actions. You can choose how often you train or whether you take performance-enhancing drugs throughout your career. You have control over your social media posts and how you present yourself in the classroom. These are the *internal* factors that come from you.

Let's return to our list, separating our factors into these two categories:

INTERNAL FACTORS   EXTERNAL FACTORS

Social media posts on your   The starting lineup (and whether
personal account   or not you are on it).
Training sessions in the gym.   Your team's performance.
Effort level in the classroom.   An injury.

Countless situations could arise, impacting who you are in the eyes of your customers. While it may feel disheartening to realize that you have no say in some of these situations, the good news is that you control a lot more than you think.

WHAT YOU CONTROL

It can be easy to get caught up in external factors and let them discourage you. This is the negative self-talk that many of us deal with. Maybe you tell yourself you'll never be chosen for that prestigious college team or that people will never follow you on social media. You might decide that a teacher dislikes you, or you believe your teammates aren't good enough to carry the team to the championship. Sometimes our focus on those external factors can even prevent us from taking the first steps to build and protect our brands. We might think: *What does it matter? It's all out of my control anyway.*

This sort of thinking is a sure-fire path to failure. This is a roadblock to becoming the best version of you. Instead of focusing on these outside factors, you must pay attention to the many, many things you *can* control. Below is a list of behaviors you can control, though it is nowhere near exhaustive.

Appearance: The way you dress, posture, and attentiveness in the classroom, who you spend time with, images on social media, body language on the sidelines, cleanliness of your locker or your car, and pride in how you "show up."

Actions: The way you speak, effort level at practice, sportsmanship in games, your handshake, how you study, participation in class, kindness, what time you show up, what you post on social media, how you spend your free time, your tenacity and grit, how you take feedback from others, and how you interact with fans.

Thoughts: Goals you set for yourself, mindfulness practices, opinions, how you speak to yourself, how you handle adversity, gratitude, aspirations and dreams, spirituality, and your attitude.

So much of your personal brand comes directly from you. You have a great deal of control over how your customers see you and the values that you choose to uphold. This is why it's so important to build your personal action plan and stick to it throughout your athletic career and your life. While it's true there will be decisions or factors that are out of your control, the majority of your choices come directly from you. *You are the biggest change-maker for your personal brand.*

WHAT YOU CAN'T CONTROL

But what do you do when a decision is truly out of your hands? We've all heard stories of high school teams disqualified from playoffs due to a single player's ineligibility or school officials failing to file the right paperwork. The COVID pandemic abruptly ended spectacular seasons for high school, college, and professional athletes nationwide. One wrong hit from an opponent and your season could end due to an injury.

These external factors all influence your brand. Sometimes, that influence is positive. If a famous alumnus makes a large donation to your school's athletic department, you may reap the rewards. But many times, external factors can hurt. Many of the examples above, from cancelled seasons to lack of playing time, and injuries, could leave your customers with a less-than-desirable perception of your brand.

Life isn't always fair, and it may seem cruel that factors outside your control can negatively impact all the hard work you've done to build the best version of yourself. It would be easy to quit in the face of adversity or blame others for your misfortune. But when external factors continue to threaten your brand, it's important to shift your focus back to what you *can* control: how you'll react. The chart below offers a few examples.

You can't control...	But you *can* control...
Your teammate's controversial social media posts	When and how you interact with your teammate
A season-ending injury	How you approach your recovery and rehab

Rejection from a potential employer	How many more applications you send out
A terrible call from a referee	How you choose to respond
A recruiter not coming to your game	Emailing the recruiter with game film

Understanding the possibility of negative external factors is half the battle. The other half is viewing the challenge as an opportunity. In this way, we can turn what we can't control into something we *can*.

THE SANDCASTLE

Imagine building a sandcastle on the beach. You carefully place each bucket of sand, meticulously design your walls and towers, dig moats, and add delicate seashell decorations to create something truly impressive. This detailed process takes both time and dedication.

But what happens next? As the tide rolls in, the gentle waves begin to erode your creation. Slowly but surely, your hard work is washed away. Or maybe, unexpectedly, a large wave crashes down, instantly destroying everything you've built.

You can think about your personal brand in the same way. It's something you cultivate with care, developing a reputation you're proud of. But if you become complacent after the initial effort, you might find your brand gradually weakening over time. Or, a significant unexpected change could hit you, altering how you are perceived. Be alert to change, or everything you've worked for could disappear.

So, what do you do if you've made a wrong decision and your brand seems permanently damaged? What do you do if you've ignored your values for a bit too long and your sandcastle is starting to erode?

It's a simple answer: you rebuild.

Determine your values. Prioritize your customers. Build your action plan. The waves of influence don't stop, and neither should your commitment to building the best you.

THE FINAL SCORE

In this chapter, we discussed internal and external factors that can affect your brand. There are many factors you can control as you work to build your brand. However, there are some things you can't control. Recognizing these internal and external factors exist is an important part of your brand management.

While external factors negatively impacting your brand can be frustrating, you can reframe those challenges into opportunities. You are the biggest changemaker for your brand, so shift your mindset to the things you can control: your appearance, your actions, and your thoughts.

Most importantly, you control your level of commitment to your Brand Action Plan. Don't stand by passively while waves of influence erode what you've built. And if you're hit with a sudden, significant change go back to the basics of what you've learned to build your brand.

CHAPTER 7 EXERCISE

1. **Internal factors that could impact your brand can be broken down into your appearance, your thoughts, and your actions.** Write down three examples under each category of internal factors that you can begin practicing today.

APPEARANCE
1.
2.
3.

THOUGHTS
1.

2.
3.

ACTIONS
1.
2.
3.

2. **Write down two external factors that could affect your brand negatively.** How will you respond?

    a. Describe the first external factor:

_____

_____

_____

_____

_____

    b. How will you respond?

_____

_____

_____

_____

_____

_____

    c. Describe the second external factor:

_____

_____

_____

_____

_____

_____

d. How will you respond?

_____

_____

_____

_____

_____

3. **Write down two external factors that could affect your brand positively.** How will you take advantage?

a. Describe the first external factor:

_____

_____

_____

_____

_____

_____

b. How will you take advantage?

_____

_____

_____

_____

_____

c. Describe the second external factor:

_____

_____

_____

_____

_____

_____

d. How will you take advantage?

_____

_____

_____

_____

_____

_____

THE *FINAL* FINAL SCORE

I wrote this book to give you the tools to create the best version of you. It's not a complicated formula, but there are very specific steps you must take to find your success. When I saw my sons navigating the complicated world of sports and school athletics, I knew I could make things easier by applying what I've learned in decades of media, public relations, and business to their experiences. I wanted to give them a step-by-step playbook to succeed in sports, school, and life. And now I'm passing that playbook on to you.

With each chapter you read, exercise you completed, and question you answered, you formed important ideas about who you are, what you value, and what you want others to see. I hope you have gained an awareness of what's important to you and understand that you are in control, even when it might feel otherwise. You have the power to take your brand in any direction you choose. All you have to do is put in the work.

So let's look back on our game plan for success:

1. All products have brand value, the intangible sum of what you feel when you experience that product. *You* are also a product, and *you* also have brand value.

2. You have different "customers" who make judgments about your brand. Know your customers and think about how you want them to feel about you.

3. Take time to determine what you want to stand for. Identify the values that build the best version of yourself.

4. Build your Brand Action Plan. Develop daily, weekly, and monthly behaviors that strengthen each of your brand values. Stick to your plan, and you won't have to tell people what you are. They will see it in your actions.

5. Understand how your brand is reflected on social media. Negative comments and questionable photos or videos may not be well-received by some of your customers. Let your brand values guide what and how you post.

6. Be prepared for your brand to change over time. Recognize changes to yourself, your customers, and your environment that can impact how you are perceived.

7. Control what you can control. Several external factors can impact your brand. But building the best version of yourself largely lies within you. You have the ability to determine your brand.

Your personal brand is an essential aspect of your athletic and academic journey. It's also a tool you can fall back on when you need to reset your intentions or challenge yourself with new goals. I hope you will see this book as the game plan to take you to the top. And by *top*, I don't mean the Olympic Games or the major leagues. You may get there, but you don't need a professional contract to find success with your personal brand. Remember, your "top" is showing the world who you are at your best.

Professional contracts end, injuries take us out of the game, we get new jobs, and move to new cities. But there's one constant amidst all of this, and that's *you*. Focus on how you present yourself to the people around you, and you will find success in whatever you set your mind to. That's what your personal brand is all about.

You likely have a playbook to help you win in competition. This is your *other* playbook. It's just as important, and now you know how to use it. Go build the best version of you in sports, school, and life.

LIST OF VALUES

Accessible	Fashionable	Passionate
Activist	Feisty	Patient
Adventurous	Flexible	Patriotic
Altruistic	Friendly	Planner
Analytical	Funny	Positive
Artistic	Generous	Problem-solving
Authoritative	Glamorous	Quiet
Bold	Hard-working	Religious
Brave	Healthy	Resourceful
Calm	Helpful	Respectful
Caring	Humble	Responsible
Charismatic	Imaginative	Serious
Clever	Innovative	Social
Collaborative	Inspirational	Spiritual
Compassionate	Introspective	Tough
Controversial	Laid back	Strong
Cooperative	Leader	Studious
Creative	Logical	Trendsetting
Decisive	Loyal	Warm
Dependable	Mature	Whimsical
Edgy	Methodical	Witty
Elegant	Musical	Worldly
Energetic	Neat	Youthful
Expert	Old-School	
	Open-minded	

This list should spark ideas as you choose the values that are important to you, but it is nowhere near exhaustive! You can and should come up with values that are not on this list.

AMIT'S BRAND ACTION PLAN

Brand Value: Resourceful Problem Solver	
Daily Actions	1. Client work (public relations or communications coaching) 2. Play games like Scrabble, Wordscapes, and Sudoku to stay in a problem-solving mindset 3. Always offer to help someone who needs assistance with a problem
Weekly Actions	1. Help clients navigate significant crisis communications issues 2. Small home maintenance project 3. Help kids with homework
Monthly Actions	1. Larger home maintenance 2. Deeper client strategy work (build communications plans, media training)

Brand Value: Expert Communicator	
Daily Actions	1. Read 2. Write 3. Follow LinkedIn articles
Weekly Actions	1. Critically watch news coverage to study how people respond in different situations 2. Read PR blogs about industry trends
Monthly Actions	1. Give a speech, training, or presentation

Brand Value: Positive People-Person	
Daily Actions	1. Be grateful 2. Look on the bright side 3. Be helpful 4. Be present
Weekly Actions	1. Give unexpected "gifts" 2. Find a moment of "awe"
Monthly Actions	1. Reconnect with an old friend or contact 2. Try to connect two colleagues

Brand Value: Devoted Family Guy	
Daily Actions	1. Spend time with family 2. Family dinners 3. Be present
Weekly Actions	1. Attend kids' games and activities 2. Coach kids' sports teams
Monthly Actions	1. Family "project" (video, vacation planning, etc.) 2. Volunteer for kids' activities

BRAND ACTION PLAN

Brand Value:	
Daily Actions	1. 2. 3.
Weekly Actions	1.

	2.
	3.
Monthly Actions	1.
	2.
	3.

BRAND ACTION PLAN

Brand Value:	
Daily Actions	1.
	2.
	3.
Weekly Actions	1.
	2.
	3.

Monthly Actions	1.
	2.
	3.

BRAND ACTION PLAN

Brand Value:	
Daily Actions	1. 2. 3.
Weekly Actions	1. 2. 3.

Monthly Actions	1.
	2.
	3.

BRAND ACTION PLAN

Brand Value:	
Daily Actions	1. 2. 3.
Weekly Actions	1. 2. 3.

Monthly Actions	1.
	2.
	3.

BRAND ACTION PLAN

Brand Value:	
Daily Actions	1. 2. 3.
Weekly Actions	1. 2. 3.

Monthly Actions	1.
	2.
	3.

NOTES

CHAPTER 1

1. "Lewis Hamilton," *F1*, 2025, https://www.formula1.com/en/information/drivers-hall-of-fame-lewis-hamilton.6TbSwzJA2miTUwtnXUHkjk.
2. Macur, Juliet, "Feeling Adrift, Biles Chooses To Step Back." *New York Times*, 28 July 2021, p. A1(L).

CHAPTER 2

1. Vecsey, George, "Setting the Gold Standard: Phelps Wins Record Eighth in Relay," *New York Times*, August 17, 2008.
2. Crouse, Karen, "Phelps Apologizes for Marijuana Pipe Photo," *New York Times*, February 2, 2009.
3. Macur, Juliet, "Photograph Costs Phelps 3 Months and a Sponsor," *New York Times*, February 6, 2009.

CHAPTER 3

1. Grez, Matias, "Brownlee brothers: Triathlete Alistair Brownlee hauls Jonny over finish line," *CNN Wire*, September 19, 2016, https://www.cnn.com/2016/09/19/sport/alistair-brownlee-jonny-brownlee-world-triathlon-series.
2. Majendie, Matt, "Jonny feels he can beat his brother next time; in association with," *London Evening Standard* [London, England], August 19, 2016, 68.
3. Steafel, Eleanor, "Alistair Brownlee: 'Mum wouldn't have been happy if I'd left Jonny behind,'" *The Telegraph*, 24 September 2016, https://www.telegraph.co.uk/health-

fitness/body/alistair-brownlee-mum-wouldnt-have-been-happy-if-id-left-jonny-b/.

4. Fleisher, Larry, "Torpedo-shaped bats draw attention after Yankees hit team-record 9 homers in rout of Brewers," *AP Online*, March 30, 2025, https://apnews.com/article/torpedo-bats-yankees-6ac6c797ea935941ed1c0d0e51a7d870.

CHAPTER 4

1. Oddo, Chris, "By the Numbers: Serena Williams, an unmatched legend," *US Open*, 3 September 2022, https://www.usopen.org/en_US/news/articles/2022-09-03/serena_williams_the_legend_by_the_numbers.html

2. Williams, Serena, "Training Like a Pro," *Masterclass.com*, https://www.masterclass.com/classes/serena-williams-teaches-tennis/chapters/training

CHAPTER 5

1. Leuzzi, John, "Who is Amir Khan? Meet McNeese basketball student manager, March Madness sensation," *USA Today Network*, 22 March 2025, https://www.usatoday.com/story/sports/ncaab/2025/03/22/amir-khan-mcneese-basketball-student-manager-march-madness/82604160007/

2. Graham, Matthew, "Amir 'Aura' Khan makes staggering amount on NIL deals on his way to NC State," *The Athlete Lifestyle*, 22 March 2025, https://www.si.com/onsi/athlete-lifestyle/business/amir-khan-mcneese-makes-staggering-amount-nil-deals-nc-state

3. Darvin, Lindsay, "Caitlin Clark and Angel Reese are Changing the Culture of Fan Engagement," 12 April 2024, https://www.forbes.com/sites/lindseyedarvin/2024/04/12/women-athletes-are-changing-the-culture-of-fan-engagement/

CHAPTER 6

1. Cohen, Kelly, "Timeline of Lance Armstrong's Career Successes, Doping Allegations, and Final Collapse," *ESPN*, 22 May 2020, https://www.espn.com/olympics/cycling/story/_/id/29177227/line-lance-armstrong-career-successes-doping-allegations-final-collapse.

2. "Armstrong Shrugs Off Doping Inquiry," *New York Times*, January 22, 2005, D7.

3. Vertuno, Jim, "Lance Armstrong faces big decision in doping case," *Associated Press*, August 23, 2012.

4. Schrotenboer, Brent, "Armstrong admits doping to Oprah," *USA Today*, January 15, 2013, 01C.

5. Levs, Josh, "Lance Armstrong's epic downfall," *CNN*, October 22, 2012, https://www.cnn.com/2012/10/22/sport/lance-armstrong-controversy.

6. Schrotenboer, Brent, "Nike Breaking livestrong link," *USA Today*, May 30, 2013, 03C.

7. Smith, Aaron and Hibah Yousuf, "Kodak files for bankruptcy," *CNN*, January 19, 2012, https://money.cnn.com/2012/01/19/news/companies/kodak_bankruptcy/index.htm.

8. Isidore, Chris, Jackie Wattles, Parija Kavilanz, "Toys 'R' Us will close or sell all US stores." *CNN*, March 15, 2018, https://money.cnn.com/2018/03/14/news/companies/toys-r-us-closing-stores/index.html.

9. Williams, Chris, "Blockbuster begins phased closure," *Daily Telegraph* [London, England], November 29, 2013, 3.

10. "Colin Kaepernick Biography", *ESPN*, https://www.espn.com/nfl/player/bio/_/id/14001/colin-kaepernick.

CHAPTER 7

1. Brennan, Christine, "Opinion: For 1980 athletes, Olympic postponement brings bittersweet memories of boycott," *USA Today*, 8 April 2020, https://www.usatoday.com/story/sports/columnist/brennan/2020/04/08/olympic-boycott-40-years-later-us-athletes/2964840001/

2. "The Olympic Boycott, 1980," *US Department of State Archive*, https://2001-2009.state.gov/r/pa/ho/time/qfp/104481.htm#:~:text=In%201980%2C%20the%20United%20States,countries%20sent%20athletes%20to%20compete.

www.ingramcontent.com/pod-product-compliance
Lightning Source LLC
Chambersburg PA
CBHW031421120626
46545CB00006B/2220